Poems By Chester

LOVE THAT FEELS

Chester L. Figures Sr.

iUniverse, Inc.
New York   Bloomington

Poems By Chester
Love that feels

iUniverse books may be ordered through booksellers or by contacting:

iUniverse
1663 Liberty Drive
Bloomington, IN 47403
www.iuniverse.com
1-800-Authors (1-800-288-4677)

ISBN: 978-1-4401-7335-6 (pbk)
ISBN: 978-1-4401-7336-3 (ebk)

Library of Congress Control Number: 2009937236

Printed in the United States of America

iUniverse rev. date: 9/25/2009

Contents

Love Expressions

WHAT KIND OF LOVE
12/19/2008

To really know true love you must know exactly what you are feeling:
Most don't know but true love is where we get most of our inner
healing.
To understand what love means you must study from the language of
the Greek:
To know why when you fall into the depths of love you are all warm
cuddly and meek.
Agape is from above where all love stems from, Storge is a natural
affection like what comes from a parent to an offspring, with this
come our first feelings of touch and you know what a good feeling
that brings.
Philia is friendship with out it we would be missing out on so many
pleasures in life. Even to explore and meet new people until we meet
some one we want to call our wife.
Eros is where we get our English word erotic. Passionate love separates
just friendships into a different category; the desire to be held and
touched in an erotic way goes far beyond friendship but takes us to a
much deeper glory.
There is nothing better than to love and be loved and experience all
kinds and keep them in their places. For those that know when they
have a good hand that is better than four aces.

Love Talk

12/19/2008

Most will listen if you talk about love, but to really discuss it you
must know it comes from above.
Most have been told by some one these words "I love you", then later
to have your heart ripped out leaving you not knowing what to do.
True love stems from our creator, but when we allow him to he loves
through us that creates more power than a nuclear generator. I'm
going to do a segment of poems on love so please don't start hating;
I'm just using my word arsenal to do a little creating.

LOVES THAT FEELS

12/19/2008

When you fall into the presents of true love, there is no mistaking it
because it is something that you can feel because it is as gentle as a
beautiful dove.
Not only can you feel love but love feels you: you draw from each
other not many have really felt this to know just a very few.
How can you feel love I hear you say: Love is alive like you are that is
why it can enrich you and have you glowing every day.
When you really get to know love you know it only has your best at
heart:
To hold it and cherish it can only be described as a gifted form of art.

TOUGH LOVE
12/19/2008

Tough love is when some one we love does things that you know will
hurt them, that is when we put our foot down and say I will help you
but not in the way that you want me too but you are still my little
gem.
My darling crack head loved one from me you ain't getting a dime,
but if you want to go to rehab I have enough time.
You can't stay at my house until you stop all of that stealing, not until
then will I put forth the effort to start our relationship healing.
I love you knuckle head that's why I am being tough, but until you
really want help things around hear are going to be rough.

IN LOVE
12/19/2008

Being in love is so very hard to explain, It is like it has you wrapped
in it and have you doing crazy stuff like walking in the rain.
It will have you talking to your self saying why I'm I doing this and
you do it any way, but down inside you are hoping for a better day.
It is good if it is the same from both sides but if you are in love by
your self you are just going along for the ride and before it is over you
will want to find a place to hide.
I'm not knocking falling in love, every one should feel it at least once
in a life time, and just pray you get the right person who will for a life
time make your heart chime.

I Didn't Plan To Do It

12/19/2008

You can't plan to fall in love it happens automatic. Most time when
you don't want it to happen it does, so don't panic.

You will say I didn't plan to do it I was just having a little fun, but it
sneaked up on you like a hostage on the run.

Love is like that, it does not play by all of the rules, when you're not a
kid any more like puppy love in school. Love is a very real thing, and
worth every moment even if sometimes it stings.

WHEN LOVE HURTS

12/19/2008

With all of the joy that it brings sometimes love hurts: that does not
mean it's not real or good but trouble comes in spurts.

If it is true love just hang on in there with the strength you have you
know you are able. You may have to jump start it again with a set of
jumper cables.

Instead of dwelling on all of the "hurtin" you may have to jump stark
raven naked from behind the bedroom curtain.

LOVE: THE HEALING BALM
12/21/2008

I would never knock medical science with all of its advances, but how much study has been put into the healing balm of love and all it enhances.

Just to hear the words I love you can sooth the spirit and the soul.

To be truly loved is far better than much silver and gold.

This is a true saying to the young and the old.

WHAT HE IS

12/21/2008

The scripture says "He that love's not knows not God for God is Love".

That's why we can safely say that all love comes from above.

When you love others you are an extension of him, that's how he lets us all know that we are his special gem.

To be truly loved is with out hypocrisy and guile, lets you know how he is who loves unconditionally with such great style.

To Really Know Him
12/21/2008
To really know him goes much farther than just going to church.
To know him personally you must know him through love and not
an angry god waiting to kill you and send you to hell or even worst.
The God I serve is a God who loves unconditionally in every entity,
and of a truth that love will last beyond infinity.

A MIND THING
12/21/2008

My Dearest darling you have captivated my mind, so let me show you
how much by being loving and kind.

True love can't be shown until it starts in the mind and reaches to the
depths of the heart, then when we enter Eros the erotic will be a work
of art.

Real love must be given body and soul, for when it is really genuine it
will make both of us completely whole.

Our love my dear reaches spirit soul and body, and it doesn't hurt my
feelings at all that you are a real hotty.

My Star
12/19/2008

My love you don't have to be from Hollywood to be my shining star.
You brighten my life with your beauty just the way you are.
The magic and the glitter of cameras and the glitter of being famous
is all good; but to reach my soul you must be the real you and let me
be the real me; that will be the shining light that the whole world will
want to see.
Let's just be real, you can be yourself at all time around me with out
being judged, it will be their problem if any one holds a grudge.
Always remember my love you will always be my star, whether we are
on a space shuttle, riding a plane or just driving in a car.

DELIGHT
12/22/2008

Just being in your presents my love is such a wonderful delight,
it is like gazing at the most beautiful scenery to hold all through
the night.   You have given me much love and hope beyond all
words; It makes my heart pound as a thousand buffalo running
as one herd.
To love you my dear is so very easy; how do I know its real love?
When I am holding you love my stomach gets all queasy.

TRANSPARENT

12/22/2008

A love that is transparent does not need any vices; instead of manipulating each other we can see who can be the nicest.
I can't promise I will never hurt you, that can't be expected not even from a parent, but one thing I can promise you is it won't be on purpose and you can see my realness because I will always be transparent.

ANOTHER CHRISTMAS

12/23/2008

Another Christmas is upon us to hopefully enjoy, some say it's just another day after shopping you could easily get annoyed.
The day is a day to share love, peace and happiness and not dwell on all the crappiness.
Look at some one and smile and wait for a smile to return. Some how we must get this message of love to every one to satisfy the spot that every one can discern.

THE ESSENCE OF LOVE
12/24/2008

The real essence of love like a magnet draws others in to you;
The more love they feel they hold to you as if you used glue.
All it takes is the slightest little bit; but the more you pour on you
couldn't beat them off with a stick.
Every one is searching for this thing called love; I guess the reason is
that it all stems from above.
From the top to the bottom, from the smallest to the largest, even
from the weakest to the greatest; the essence of love is being sought
after from the earliest of time until the latest.

WHEN IT IS NOT THERE
12/24/2008

When true love is not there it leaves such a great void; sometimes it
feels like you have been hit with an asteroid.
You search and search for it really to no avail; then when you can't
find it is like you have been kicked in the tail.
Men blame it on the woman and the woman blames it on the man;
This thing called love none of us will completely understand.
When it is there you will know it and surely show it; but when it is
not there every thing you do it seems that you blow it.

THE FEELING OF BELONGING
12/24/2008

One thing love does it makes you feel like you belong; it lets you feel excepted even if you are wrong.

When others don't except you just the way you are; it is an uncomfortable thing to get nit picked while they look for every mar. When you hear these words "I love you' It makes you relax and feel I really belong; If you have watched the old show on TV you don't have to worry about being gonged.

MERGING PAIN
12/24/2008

In the merging of two lives there has to be pain; You've done things
one way for so longs and the other has done theirs some times the
words that are said leaves an ugly stain.
When it is true love all things will work together; and given time and
understanding you can make it through the bad weather.
If things get bad remember its merging pains; just chill for a moment,
kiss and make up and hold hands while walking through the rain.
Remember if pain comes from merging that you get from the start;
just think of how much pain will come when you try to pull it apart.

THROUGH THE EYES OF LOVE

12/24/2008

When seeing things through the eyes of love, things seem to be better
and more pleasing as the tenderness of a dove.

When things seem to be unpleasant and you feel like old sergeant
McGruff; look through the eyes of love and you will realize it's not all
of that tuff.

Take things in stride and go along for the ride, look through the eyes
of love and forget about that puffed up pride.

LADIES LOVE

I love the ladies, as much as any man, There is room for one by my
side.
But I'm not one for going along for the ride.
When we work together we both come alive.
I don't need a door mat to walk on,
just one who loves me with whom I can get along.
We must work together that's the way God planned it.
For out of Gods plan we will both regret it.

BEAUTIFUL ROSE
9/28/2008

The flower most intriguing to my eye is the beautiful rose.
It has softened many hearts and set the stage for many life times of happiness
And confirmed many apologies well you know how that goes.
When men can't say what is on their mind just a thought of a beautiful flower has set the stage for wonderful romance.
With out them most would not even get a second glance.
I tell you just one beautiful rose has gotten me a second chance.
The rose only breaks the ice, your words after will seal the deals
The rose has even brought out my poetic skills.
That's enough of words I will go and buy some for my beautiful lady of choice.
Maybe we will both gaze at each other with love as we both rejoice.

Reverence

EARTH CREATION

What does God think of his earth creation?
I wonder what it will be like for the rest of the duration.

It's hard to fathom the way things are.
But what does He think looking down from afar.

He can't be pleased with so much hate deceit and least of all disease.
With just the things I've been through it keeps me on my knees.

I know Jesus has a better view than me of this world's strife;
for he sets high and looks low so he knows how to separate the good
from the bad as cutting with a knife.

The sheep on the right, the goats on the left;
Many will say Lord, Lord didn't I do.
But Jesus will say depart from me. Your works was done for know one
else but you.

Too many way's to bless

My God has too many ways' to bless,
for me to set around and worry about this mess.

Jesus has promised me a great blessing,
How it's going to come I won't waste my time guessing.

I've given him all of my life,
I don't really know why I have to go through such toil and strife.

The judger has judged the liar has lied.
Lest I can help it they won't know if I have cried.

I've never met most of these people who are lashing out at me.
If I knew them I would go and talk to them firmly but yet nice as can
be.

I'm really getting tired of the whole world messing.
Maybe it's because they have left me guessing.

I know nothing for sure but Jesus is coming.
Then the whole wide world will know he's the alive and the true God.
If they only knew how much I love him they wouldn't call me odd.

I'm only guilty of living my life as I do every day.
It's not my fault someone has places bugs on me or around me to see
and hear every thing I do or say

I think the way to cope is not to change a thing , just live my life as I
do all the time.
Maybe you can help me think of a word to put here that may rhyme

GOD'S ELECT

When you set out to destroy Gods Elect you only make them stand more erect.

What could make men try to destroy another especially one who he should call his brother.

I've always believed that if you cant say something to a mans face it shouldn't be said. Especially those who say they are spirit led.

You have followed ever move I've made for over two years to try to prove me a sinner.

If you would asked me I would have told you I was But I've been washed in the blood of Jesus and now I'm a winner.

I can truly say in my past I've did a lot of things I'm not proud of, but now I can say proudly I rest in his love.

You have treated me unfair I will always believe. Lest you repent you will get caught in your own weave.

I think you purposely tried to run me crazy.

I guess I could fake a good one and get an SSI check, but then you would call me lazy.

I keep hearing you say that I must be depressed.

I stop and think what is all this mess. It must be an extremely light case of the ugly you see.

I can't help that but what's inside is bubbly as can be.

A Prayer

God please let your will be done.
You know all about me and you know I never have from anything
run.
I know things have changed I feel it in the air.
No one has talked to me yet about anything.
To guess at this point I wouldn't dare.
I will do your will what ever it may be.
I will trust in you totally because you are the Big He.
I don't know what tomorrow may bring.
I'm ready to worship and serve you for you are my King.

Broken Spirit

A broken spirit who can mend especially hurt brought on by
carnal men?
When you say you are spiritual and you reach out to hurt. That's
as carnal as the man you call a flirt.
Only God can judge the heart and spirit of a man. The one you
say will fall usually is the one who will stand.
There is a fine line between the two. One mans spirituality is
another's carnality.
But the almighty knows when you are living in true reality.
You can fake being deep or you can fake being shallow. But God
sees all the way to the bone marrow.
You can't fool the Big He with your want to be deep self.
When Jesus comes back don't fool around and get left.

STOLEN LIFE

When your life has been stolen by manipulative means;
All you have left is God and the memory of being called dean.
When all have forsaken you and you don't know who to trust.
Having a strong faith I God is an absolute must.
When the folks on your job or at church have a hidden agenda,
Then you must hide yourself in Jesus for he is the only one who
will never offend ya.
Sometimes it feels as if I'm even forsaken by him.
Then he tells me I'm his precious gem.

The Inner Self
12/14/2008

When all else fails you must rely on your inner self, because most
time when you are down others will want to completely take you off
of the shelf.

When you know there is much good in you and it seems that there is
no one to help you bring it to the forefront, that is when you draw on
you inner self and like they do in football just drop back and punt.
Most don't realize that the inner self is a most powerful tool, a tool
that you can't learn to use by going to school.

When you are all alone it brings out strength that you did not know
you had. When you are faced to do things with out help it lets you
know you're not at all bad.

This is not at all excluding the true and living God. For in your inner
self is where his Spirit chooses to abide. His Spirit living in your spirit
makes it a spectacular ride.

In this world when you're faced with being all alone, learn to rely on
your inner self and know you are tough all the way to the bone.

BLESSEDNESS

12/14/2008

While resting in his blessedness none of us can boast that we are all
of that, if you have good sense you would know that it is not you that
does the doing, you are just a spot in time I can even call you a brat.
Blessedness comes only from the Big He; it is only his favor that rest
upon you that allows you even to be.

If you have found divine favor with Him cherish the moment, Give
all praise and adoration to him for it is a gift from the Big He, You
couldn't even afford the down payment so just say thank you Jesus for
choosing me..

Basque in the radiance of his blessedness for the warmth of that light
feels better than lying on the most beautiful beech in the sun that he
has created.

If any one tells you there is something better besides heaven you tell
them the mess they are talking about is surely over rated.

COMPLETENESS
12/16/2008

Most folks want happiness but don't really know what it is. We get most of our ideas of happiness from a thing called show biz.

What we really are in search of is completeness some how to become whole without being judged in weakness.

The best way to know completeness is when you are content; and some how managing to cover all the bases and not worry about the rent.

Completeness as a far cry from winning when we compete; but its feeling good about your self just to know you are complete.

SHOUTING

12/14/2008

From the mountain top you feel like shouting the name of the Big
He.
He is the one in charge and will avenge me from the earthly powers
that be.
They hurt me to the depths of my soul by attacking me when I was
minding my own business, not bothering any one just chilling and
taking care of the things in my world with easiness.
They put me in contest and did not even tell me when I won, Just
let me go on and even had the nerve to try to belittle me with their
would be shun.
I'm shouting on the house top and don't mind saying it.
These people have angered the almighty God and he's on my side so
they better get with it.

CHRISTMAS
12/25/2008

Another Christmas day and it seems that we are all healthy; with all
of the blessings from him probably another day I will think about
being wealthy.

I am grateful for all he has dome for me in this life; because the good
always out weigh the toil and the strife.

I'm not concerned about gifts to open because he has already given
me the greatest gift of all; that is salvation through his name and a
promise to catch me before I fall.

REAL HURT
Written September 7th 2000

Real hurt comes when it is not expected.
Especially from those through time a relationship has been erected.

Through the years what you saw was a smile.
Then suddenly you found it was all guile.

Real hurt comes from those you love
You no the ones that you expect to return the same love.
Then suddenly you find that the only true is agape from above.

I imagined what Christ my Lord must have felt.
When he hung on the cross with the treatment he was dealt

He said forgive them Lord for they know not what they do.
He whispered in my ear and told me he expect the same from me and
you.

SCREAM FROM THE BELLY OF HELL
Written December 2003

Out of the belly of hell I cried Lord save me.
But when I cried only a great peace he gave me.
He said soon you will be out of this great trouble;
I'll even help you clean up the rubble.
While you are in the middle of this great storm;
He say's just rest in My everlasting arms and hold true to form.
I don't know why I've had to go through such a thing.
But I know that my God is able to remove the pain from the sting.
I wish I could say I've did every thing just right.
But I know I haven't while going through this plight.
While going through this storm it feels like every thing is going to
break up.
Or that you're in a bad dream and soon you will wake up.
Some how you gain a little strength to continue to run this race,
With the encouragement he gives you realize it's only his grace.

WHAT THE FUTURE HOLDS

I don't know what the future holds.
But knowing my savior it has to be big and bold.
I've been in the dark for a long time now;
with only the light from heaven and the glory of Jesus to endow.
I don't know why I've been picked out to be picked on.
I know someone has the answer and all they have to do is pick up the
phone.
I have a settled peace deep down within now.
Because Jesus has proven himself to me and others and to him I bow.
One thing I know, I know that I'm saved and been washed in his
blood. I also know that I've been born again, so the trials can't kill me
even if they came in like a flood for when the enemy comes in, Like a
flood the spirit of the Lord will lift up a standard against him.
When you really don't know who your enemy is; you just give it to
God and say reverently please take care of all of them.

THE GREATER GOOD

What could have been used for the greater good has been toyed
with and manipulated to weaken the hearing of the true voice of our
creator;.
and water thrown on every thing as deadly as that from an old
radiator.
When in a never ending cycle it will make you seek God more or pull
out the old rifle.
When things haven't been fair from the start;
Its like someone has you by the heart trying to pull it apart.
Who knows what the future holds. Only the Big He knows.
When you feel his sadness and how far we've drifted, Lets get back to
him for we are already at all time lows.

AFRICAN AMERICAN VIEW

"In this section many of these poems were written on or near the birthday of the Reverend Doctor Martin Luther King Jr. for celebrations honoring him and his work. Please understand they were not written to inspire racism or hate of any kind".

PROUD BUT NOT PREJUDICE
Written February 28th 1999
We must teach our young people not to be prejudice but yet proud.
Nor can we walk around with our head in a cloud.

There are things that happen that could cause you to be prejudice
But your dignity must rise to the top and know that all men are not this
Ridiculous.
There is good and bad people in all races; but don't let your name or actions
Be involved in these traces.
You can be proud of who and what you are and not be prejudice,
And not be named with this world's indifference.

SHATTERED DREAMS
February 28th 1999

The dreams of a black man are often shattered
And too many times his family scattered.

I asked the Almighty why is this woe brought on the black man.
And how can we surpass this woe and be able to stand.

The Almighty replied to me, as long as I'm in charge your dignity will
raise to the top.
One day I will make all things equal and no mans dignity will
another be able to stop.

Until I make all things equal hold your head high.
It won't be long if even in the sweet by and by.

So until that time just take it on the chin.
Then say to your self another ignorant soul then give a slight grin.

There is no way to end this sometimes I say.
But remember with the Almighty there is a better day.

STRIVE TO BE BETTER
Written February 25th 1996

We must strive to be better, is the black mans fate.
For just being equal you will come up late.
For the man of no color can excel being average.
The man of color must be above for his short comings are blown into
cadaver age.
I must say the chore to be black is such a privilege.
To excel in this world we must press pass our pilgrimage.
Any one can be average both black and white.
But the successful man of color has pressed pass this plight.
You may be a lawyer or you may be a street sweeper.
Just remember that the Almighty God is our keeper.
So I'm proud of who and what I am.
For I was made this way proudly I say by the great I Am That I Am.

THE BLACK MANS STAND

When you look at me you see a black man.
But you really should see much more if you can.

You may see a man who speaks fluent Ebonics.
Or someone setting around listening to stereo phonics

The strength of a black man is not only his back.
He also my friend is strong in the mind.
The real black man is also very kind.
We've been belittled by the white man but also our own kind.

You call me militant if I take a stand against being oppressed,
then won't give me a job setting at a desk.

You will elevate the black woman above the black man
It makes me wonder if you would take advantage of her in some
ungodly way because you can.

You must have something to fear because you won't let me be equal.
It seems were living a never-ending sequel.

Believe I'm not trying to be greater than you in this crazy race.
I only want to take my God given place.

WHEN IS A MAN FREE?

10/10/2008

When is a man free if treated like a toy or at 53 yet being treated like
a boy?
Is a man free when bound by mans opinion when they tie you up
with words and red tape as tight as can be?
Is a man free when alienated and treated like an outsider in his own
country?
If that is not bad enough they want to depict you as a fool
or an illiterate person who hasn't been to school.
When is a man free when they can't put you behind bars but they
lock you up so you can't reach for the stars?

Life's Evaluation

MEASURING WORTH
12/25/2008

How can I measure what I am worth? It can't be measured by all I
have accumulated on this earth.

When you don't hear many accolades about the things you have done;
you have to remember it was not you that caused the victory to be
won.

To measure self worth you can't look for pats on the back; just
imagine if by chance you was not here anymore how many people's
life would be in lack.

If the Almighty had not let you live your life on this earth; how many
people would not exist or have what they have as they try to tally
their own life to know what they are worth.

Sometime you have to encourage yourself and know if you don't hear
it from any one that your worth is far above the dollars you can count
and the things you have bought in stores; just remember that our
Creator has used you to be a blessing to others and open many doors.

Think about it how many people's life would be effected if you weren't
here; even if they don't say it if they are thinking people they will
hold you very dear.

THINGS YOU JUST CAN'T DO
12/17/2008
You can't make people like you and certainly you can't make people
love you, especially when they think they are above you.
Who told them they were all of that, it makes you want to hit them
with a base ball bat.
All of the signs a finger on the nose, a finger in the nose God forbid
some of the other signs; I'll tell them what to do with the water hose.
They think you are too stupid to know what's going on, with all the
words of riddles flying back and forth like playing ping pong.
A sneeze a yarn while they treat you like some animal in a barn,
sometimes you want to nit their mouth shut with a whole skein of
yarn.
Believe me my friends it is a lot you want to do but just can't do,
when you want to hold up a standard for the one who made you.

POLLUTED

12/14/2008

When the heart of a person is completely polluted, it makes you
wonder why and how it got so deeply rooted.
When dealing with an entire society that from the top is corrupt, you
call on the living God and make sure you are out of the way before it
erupts.
They picked at me first with out a cause; I was minding my own
business with my life in a slight pause.
So I don't mind putting my foot where it hurts, they should be more
careful who you belittle their worth.
When you get sick and tired of being sick and tired, you will stomp
them in the ground along with who ever they hired.

SMILE OR FROWN
12/14/2008

When the outside world sees you what do they see, most times we
allow then to see what we want them to see, a face that smiles.
But to know what is really inside we would frighten them for what's
on the outside is mostly guile.
On the outside it is a smile but inwardly a very sad frown, especially
when you think you are perceived as a rodeo clown.
Why is it we can't be real and show and be what we are, instead of
trying to show the world that I have it all together and can afford my
large new luxury car?
Life is not always fair and has thrown us all curves, but when it does
we have to swing and hit a home run and show the word we still have
our nerve.
The more I think on it I know it is really a good thing, to be able to
smile through it all and show good tidings with what ever life brings.
The old antic " a smile is just a frown turned upside down" only goes
to show us that the way we position our mouth does not always show
what is inside.
Just watch my smile and come along for the ride.

A Better Day

12/13/2008

I'm looking for a better day, At least that's what I have been promised any way.

I don't want to be like Otis Redding and just setting on the dock of the bay. "Yes my fried Just setting on the dock of the bay wasting time".

Waiting for my hair to turn gray, with all that is with in me that would be a crime.

I'm looking for a brighter day when my smile will be real, and know one will have to wonder "what is the big deal".

When that day comes it will be good for all, and no one can deny me God's call.

Then I won't have to depend on U-Haul to move me along, but will have the money to get things done and not worry about being done wrong.

I'm looking for a brighter day, when all men are equal, well any way that is what they say.

EDUCATION
May 19th 1996

Education is important to excel in this world, for with out or you may miss that great pearl.

What pearl you may ask, the pearl of a great price; one that can only be attained but by great sacrifice.

They say we are equal to all other men: but to attain the same thing we must work harder than them.

I commend any one who attains an education; for you have sacrificed more to achieve your chosen occupation.

My hats off to you for all the hard work you have done; for of a truth your blessings have just begun.

Hurts and Pain

PART OF LIFE
12/9/2008

Shattered dreams are a part of life, that is why they call it toil and
strife.
You never know what to expect, not even from those who you think
are standing erect.
Life has not been good to me, but I've played the hand that I have
been dealt.
Sometimes a good bluff can win, or at least stop a dwindling melt.
See the trick work of the evil doer. They pierce to the heart as with a
skewer.

A Better Day

12/13/2008

I'm looking for a better day, At least that's what I have been promised
any way.

I don't want to be like Otis Redding and just setting on the dock of
the bay. "Yes my fried Just setting on the dock of the bay wasting
time".

Waiting for my hair to turn gray, with all that is with in me that
would be a crime.

I'm looking for a brighter day when my smile will be real, and know
one will have to wonder "what is the big deal".

When that day comes it will be good for all, and no one can deny me
God's call.

Then I won't have to depend on U-Haul to move me along, but will
have the money to get things done and not worry about being done
wrong.

I'm looking for a brighter day, when all men are equal, well any way
that is what they say.

DISAPPOINTMENTS

12/13/2003

Life comes with so many disappointments, for these types of wounds
there is no healing ointment.

A word of encouragement here and a word of encouragement there
really help, but at the end of the day when no one is around you still
have the bruises and whelps.

Life's disappointments don't happen every day, but they sneak up on
you and say remember me, I may be passing through but my scar is
here to stay.

When you have too many it is not hard to get over, you start to
wonder who stole all the leaves off my four leaf clover.

If I could afford it I would just leave, and drive this earth in a new
Land Rover.

SMILE OR FROWN

12/14/2008

When the outside world sees you what do they see, most times we
allow then to see what we want them to see, a face that smiles.
But to know what is really inside we would frighten them for what's
on the outside is mostly guile.
On the outside it is a smile but inwardly a very sad frown, especially
when you think you are perceived as a rodeo clown.
Why is it we can't be real and show and be what we are, instead of
trying to show the world that I have it all together and can afford my
large new luxury car?
Life is not always fair and has thrown us all curves, but when it does
we have to swing and hit a home run and show the word we still have
our nerve.
The more I think on it I know it is really a good thing, to be able to
smile through it all and show good tidings with what ever life brings.
The old antic " a smile is just a frown turned upside down" only goes
to show us that the way we position our mouth does not always show
what is inside.
Just watch my smile and come along for the ride.

WOUNDED
12/14/2008

Wounded by friendly fire hurts just as much, when the incoming bullet is from someone you know it is like a fine expensive vase being knocked off the china hutch.

You will always wonder if this was done on purpose but down inside you know friendship is irreplaceable, so you look over their actions and not look into what is really traceable.

The wound is yet there and the pain of healing has to begin, but you will probably question their loyalty until the end.

Not Wanted
12/14/2008

When you know you are not wanted by the earthly powers that be.
You must learn to rely only on the Big He.
When I speak of the Big He I am speaking of the Almighty God, the Creator of the earth.
He is the only one who knows what his souls are worth.
I have been pushed into only relying on him because from the top down in this place they are corrupt as can be.
They have their wise contest but the outcome is fixed. They set you up to try to get you out of the mix.
The Big He has reveled to me their numbers scheme. That's why I don't mind cursing them, only he can say if they are too corrupt to redeem.
The low down dirty dogs just ain't no good. It makes you want to put your foot right where you should.

WORDS OF DEATH
12/15/2008

I won't entertain words or thoughts of death, because the Creator has
too much for me to do and he promised me good health.
Along with good health he will also give me my share of wealth.
It's a horrible feeling when it feels like those closest to you want you
to die. They only want you around for with out you they cant get a
piece of the pie.
They steel your ideas and claim them for them self, and want you to
be something small like the Keebler Elf.

ANOTHER JAB

12/15/2008

With every passing day somehow they seem to get in another jab,
while you are being treated like a study in some science lab.
Another jab another lash with someone's tongue, the only vent that
you are given is breathing in much air until it fills both lungs.

WHAT IS HAPPINESS?
12/15/2008

The great question for today is what is happiness? I really don't know because much of my life has been filled with scrappiness'

You want to be able to laugh and enjoy like you see others do, but as soon as you try you get a sharp dagger in the back with words like skip you.

Happiness must be something that you can only reach for; as soon as you think you have it things fall through the floor.

Somebody tell me what is this word called happiness? Is it having lots of money, having someone to hold and say I love you or a combination of both. Someone help me in this area I really need growth.

FACING THE CHALLENGE
12/15/2008
Whether you want to or not you must face the challenge, or down in you very soul you will feel like it has been scavenged.

The challenge is sometimes just getting some one off your back. If they want to ride let them ride something else or knock them on their stack.

You have to tell them if you keep on riding you are going to loose a few teeth, you already look bad enough why put us through more grief.

ONE FAIR HAND
12/15/2008

Sometimes you find your self crying somebody please deal me a fair
hand. Instead of getting help someone shoots you with a rubber band.
One fair hand somebody please deal the cards. A full house, a royal
flush four aces any thing to get me into good graces.

If nothing else deal me a hand I can give a good bluff. Don't leave me
standing here with no cards not even one to hide in my cuff.

Hey all I ask for was one good hand. I promise I won't make too big
of a grand stand.

WHEN HURT DON'T STOP
11/1/2008

When each day goes by and no one will talk to you then what do you do.

When you cry inside with a camouflage of goodness on the outside knowing it hurts but you go along for the crazy ride.

I guess when you know they are trying to make you look like a fool, and you know how to get back but all you can think of is the golden rule.

When dealing with a judging demon all I know to do is give it something to judge.

Maybe it will consume its self in its own judgments then it's all I can do to not hold a grudge.

They have wounded me terribly by cutting me left and right. Instead of stopping they pour salt in the wounds. It makes me wonder why I have to suffer and go through this plight.

When hurt don't stop you find subtle ways to try to make things stop. You put your own life in jeopardy because there is no one you can trust not even a cop.

The thing you don't understand is I have truly been born again. So to enjoy a make shift sin is impossible so let me stretch things a little thin and make others smile then maybe you cant see what you have done to me within. When hurt don't stop you learn to live with it and with all that is with in you try to muster enough courage to let life began again.

WHO KNOWS
12/2/2008

Who knows where this is leading to; it makes you wonder if any one
knows what to do.
I don't know what the future holds, but my life will be big and bold.
I am middle age my friends and not old. What I have inside is more
precious than silver and gold.
Believe me people the half has never been told.
They won't break me what ever they do. God has greater things for
me
than walking around in an old work shoe.

PLAINLY SEEN

When you can plainly see all the guile, plots and scheme,.
All you can do is give it to God who controls all and writes the main theme.
When some have tried to change the very plan of God,
They dream up wicked plots and don't even think its odd.
The creator sees and he knows all and he always catches me before I fall.
I didn't ask for this trial
but a keen sense of Gods presents is all around me and that you can truly file.

FIXED FIGHT

What do you do when you're a winner but the fight is fixed.
When you know you've been loyal and did you're very best.
You know you should be active but you see them systematically trying
to put you to rest.
God I've always given you my all and treated men with dignity and
tried to be fair.
But everyone you deal with is blowing smoke in the air.
To be truthful about being right know one cares.
It's all about protecting their own self.
They have their signs and codes to act and react to your every move.
As they are judging me the almighty is judging them.
I believe they have slipped into a bad grove.

STOLEN LIFE

When your life has been stolen by manipulative means;
All you have left is God and the memory of being called dean.
When all have forsaken you and you don't know who to trust.
Having a strong faith I God is an absolute must.
When the folks on your job or at church have a hidden agenda,
Then you must hide yourself in Jesus for he is the only one who will
never offend ya.
Sometimes it feels as if I'm even forsaken by him.
Then he tells me I'm his precious gem.

GAME WITH NO RULES

Some one please explain the rules of this crazy game.
If I had my way no one will have to live with pain or shame.
What's going on all I've asked is for someone to talk to me and put me in the know.
You would be surprised how well I get with the flow.
I'm not at all blind I can see sometimes too much.
I need someone to talk to me and confirm what I see.
I won't tell you I'm happy about all of this. I won't know until it's over how good or haw bad it's affected me.
I don't know who to trust. You see them smile in your face then you feel a knife go in your back with a great thrust.
When you look at me you see a nice guy. But what you really see is a man with a heart as big as Texas, but friendship I shouldn't have to buy.
I try to always be kind that's just the way I am.
I pray a little comes back without it being a scam.
Under the surface there is a man who loves his God who totally rely on him to fight his battles. Yes I can handle myself in a fight but more than likely I won't for God has done just fine until now. He has kept me through the night.

WORLD OF FROGS

When you live in a world of frogs
You pick up the language
And say ribbit.
You want to swim like a graceful fish
But
They won't give you any space
Not even a tidbit.
You want to swim with the grace of a big sea bass
But
Instead you're called low class
Or
Sometimes even a Jack ass.
I'm only being humorous in a rhyme
So don't take it personal.
I'm only pulling words out of my word arsenal.
I'm only playing tonight
So don't get too uptight.
This is the way I keep from getting too heavy.
And keep the tear dam from breaking its levy.

TAKING IT IN STRIDE

I'm taking it all in stride, hoping that all will work out right so that
we can hold our head up with Godly pride.

Life is not always' fair, especially when you're living your life in the
media air.

When no one will talk to you to tell the rules of this crazy game,
instead point the finger and say who do I blame?

Every one wants to say I'm right even at the cost of being wrong.

When we stand before the almighty God then I wonder if he will let
us sing our song.

CRY FOR PRIVACY

How am I supposed to start a new or kindle an old relationship with the whole world watching?

It's not the sweet tender kisses that I would give her that I would be ashamed of. It is you out there laughing because my knees are knocking.

It's been so long sense I have been in the dating game Ill be done went back to the 1920s to get some lines.

"As long as the grass grows around the stump, I'll be your sugar lump"

"Ain't nothing boiling but the peas in the pot, and it wouldn't be boiling if the water wasn't hot"

"As long as the wind blows through the trees, don't make me beg and have to say please"

I'm kidding of course because my mack ain't tired.

I'm really trying to live a good life.

I don't want to bring any one in to this toil and strife.

Most may think I want to marry the first moment I meet a girl.

Not so I really want some one to be my friend first, maybe hold my hand and a light kiss at first. Then if the chemistry is there when the time is right we can together go out of this world.

The whole world seems to be built up around money and sex.

If I only had some one who really had my back I can do what it takes when it's time to go triple x.

Half of the ministers of the world probably just fainted. So what Its time to deal with some of the false pictures you have painted.

I know the bible teaches that we should marry before having sex.

After I'm married its not your business if I want one x or three,

This is only a poem so please I don't like the way you are looking at me.

Please give me back my privacy that you have taken.

If you really want to know what I do let me write it in a book;

Before you get to page ten I will have you shaken.

By the time you get to page twenty you will be already shook.

NINTH ANNIVERSARY
October 1996

It's been nine years sense I began our ministry at V. T.
Sometime I feel like it's my destiny
Sometimes I feel it really shouldn't be.
By his grace God sends encouragement;.
And places us back on the path of his divine intent.
I must say in our years here we've had some good times.
For when the Spirit of the Lord comes in, every thing rhymes.
I can't say I felt great all the nine years.
For some of the time I was almost in tears.
The good times has always out weighed the bad.
Where the glory of God is, things soon turn to make us glad.
Victory Temple we have so much work to do.
That's why we must stick together like glue.
You may not understand every decision I make.
Just know in your heart God leads us in the steps that we take.
The Steps of a good man are ordered by the Lord.
To be slothful or lazy we just can't afford.
I know I tread in the pastors rank.
Please except my sincere thanks.

POINT OF NOT KNOWING
12/24/2008

Well my friend when you're at the point of not knowing what to do.
That's not the time to throw up both hands and say I'm through.

Just put all your trust in the almighty God and
even though to do so most people will call you odd.

When you dig in both heals and say I just won't quit.
For down in side you know the almighty is going to bring you out of
this horrible pit.

Don't be surprised when I go to the top;
for when Jesus really works is when   men think you're a flop.

I don't know what tomorrow may bring. But regardless to how bad it
may get
To the Almighty God it just ain't no thing.

I would have things much different if it were left up to me.
But that wouldn't give much glory to the GREAT BIG HE.

As long as I hang on in there I know things has to get better;
if I hold on in the storm and turbulence of this bad weather.

I know God is able to bring me and all men out.
But it's hard to go through and not pout.

It's hard to go through with a stiff upper lip.
When you're entire life, your family, your chosen career even your
character some are trying to flip.

I know I haven't gone through all of my trials as I should.
Maybe If I had an encouraging word from someone face to face
maybe I could.

When I'm under pressure not only does your strength show but also
your weakness.
I know I'm working on mine to show a little more meekness

THE LAST STRETCH

12/14/2008

The last stretch of a race is hardest to run, by then you are feeling the
pain from every pounding step till now and from the starting gun.
The reason you run the race is to win, but before it is over with every
deep breath that you take you wonder why I even begin.
With the finish line in view you know you can't stop, but with each
time you fill your lungs with oxygen you wonder if they are going to
pop.
When in a long distance race you wonder if you paced your self
correctly, by now you hope that you can make it to the finish line and
still be standing erectly.
The finish line is in view and you know you are on the last stretch. In
your mind you know that many have made it to this point and still
did not make it because they had to stop and retch and on a stretcher
they had to be fetched.
Running your best you know it ain't over till it's over. At this point
you will take any help if even from a four leaf clover.
All of a sudden you get what they call the second wind, and you
realize at this point not only is the pain of enduring, breathing and
taking each step, but always at the end of the last stretch is the finish
line, when you get there it will be worth all of your effort, toil and
time.

MESSAGE IF HOPE

Faith in the midst of the storm
I wrote this more than twenty years ago not
Knowing how much I would need it today

The Hebrew writer defines the word faith as the substance of thing hoped for and the evidence of things not seen. Although we as saints realize that by faith we can receive from God the things we ask of him, but sometimes we fail to realize that when our faith is most needed is in the midst of the storm. It is always much easier to look back and see how God has brought you through, than it is to look forward and wonder how you are going to get through. Many times we only look at faith as the actual receiving of our blessing, but faith is needed before the blessing comes. As a result of believing God in the midst of the storm the storm passes building our faith to an even higher level in God. Many time we read about the old patriarchs how they had faith in God and received blessings from him. Many times we don't realize that before the blessing came the suffering that they went through. As a result of their faith in the midst of the storm the blessing came upon them. We must always remember that God will always keep his promises to us and he promised never to leave us or forsake us. The word of God tells us that he is a very present help in times of trouble. Remember faith is the substance of things hoped for and the evidence of things not seen.

"THE POET "
Chester L. Figures, Sr.

The poems that I write are inspired by many things in life, from the happiest of times to the very saddest. Life has taken me from extreme highs to extreme lows and I chose to use this forum to hopefully brighten others life and to share love with others and advise that all of us has had both good and bad times but our low moments can be the catapult that can spring us to our highs.

I was born in Bakersfield, California and raised in Buttonwillow California a small farming town about 30 miles west of Bakersfield. Calvin and Carless Figures my parents were good hearted solid people and I am blessed to have been raised by them who put a sound value system in my siblings and me.

For many years I have maintained two careers in actuality one has supported the other. My career of choice was that of a Christian Minister where I was senior pastor of a small to moderate congregation and evangelized through out the United Stated and abroad. I also maintained a career in and around the petroleum industry from production of oil products to delivery of petroleum products as a professional driver. For the first time in many years I am not pasturing but pursuing avenues of sharing the good news and making others smile through my writing and oratory skills.

Angelic Figures and I as husband and wife has shared in upbringing of four sons and two daughters Chester Jr., Chester L. Jr., Calvin, William, Alicia and Candice. Each of these is talented and gifted in very different ways.

The past 7 years I have resided in San Antonio Texas the home of the four time world champion San Antonio Spurs basket ball team and the Historical Alamo.

www.ingramcontent.com/pod-product-compliance
Lightning Source LLC
Chambersburg PA
CBHW031303280526
45784CB00004B/1972